ذات يوم ، قالت المرأة العجوز لكلبيها: «لقد حان الوقت كي أزور إبنتي، ابقيا هنا حتى أعود».
ثم حزمت حقيبتها ومضت في طريقها.

One day, she told her dogs, "It's time for me to visit my daughter. Stay here until I return."
She packed her bag and went on her way.

لم تقطع المرأة العجوز مسافة طويلة في الغابة حتى قابلت ثعلباً.
لما رأها الثعلب زمجر قائلاً: «بوري بوري، أريد أن آكُلكِ».

She hadn't gone far into the forest when she met a fox.
"Buri, Buri, I want to eat you," he snarled.

قالت العجوز: «أيها الثعلب، من الأفضل أن لا تأكل امرأة نحيفة مثلي».
إنتظر حتى أعود من عند إبنتي، وحينئذ سأكون جميلة وسمينة».
زمجر الثعلب قائلاً: «بوري بوري، سوف آكُلللكِ عندما تعودين».

"Oh fox, you don't want to eat a thin Buri like me. Wait until I return
from my daughter's, then I'll be nice and fat."
"Buri, Buri, when you return, I shall eat you," snarled the fox.

واصلت المرأة العجوز رحلتها حتى قابلت نمراً.
لما رآها النمر زمجر قائلاً: «بوري بوري، أريد أن أكُلكِ».

The old woman continued her journey until she met a tiger.
"Buri, Buri, I want to eat you," he growled.

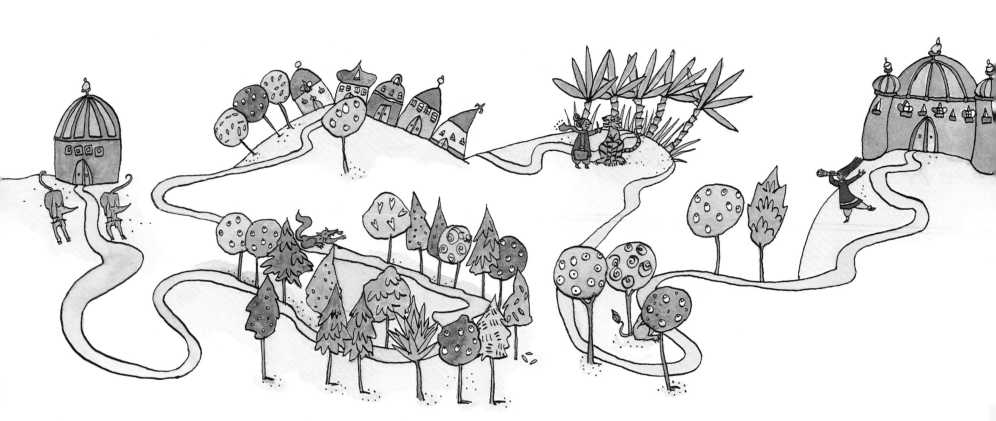

قالت العجوز: «أيها النمر، من الأفضل ان لا تأكل امرأة نحيفة مثلي، إنتظر حتى أعود من عند إبنتي، حينئذ سأكون جميلة وسمينة».

زمجر النمر قائلاً: «بوري بوري، سوف آكُلكِ عندما تعودين».

"Oh tiger, you don't want to eat a thin Buri like me. Wait until I return from my daughter's, then I'll be nice and fat."

"Buri, Buri, when you return, I shall eat you," growled the tiger.

مضت المرأة في طريقها مرة أخرى حتى قابلت أسداً.
لما رأها الأسد زأر وقال: «بوري بوري، أريد أن آكُلكِ».

The old woman went on her way again until she met a Lion.
"Buri, Buri, I want to eat you," he roared.

ردت العجوز قائلة: «أيها الأسد، من الأفضل ان لا تأكل امرأة نحيفة مثلي.
إنتظر حتى أعود من عند إبنتي، حينئذ سأكون جميلة وسمينة».
زأر الأسد وقال: «بوري بوري، سوف آكُلكِ عندما تعودين».

"Oh lion, you don't want to eat a thin Buri like me. Wait until I return
from my daughter's, then I'll be nice and fat."
"Buri, Buri, when you return, I shall eat you," roared the lion.

وأخيراً وصلت المرأة العجوز الى منزل إبنتها ثم قالت:
«إبنتي... حبيبتي... لقد كانت رحلتي إليك مخيفة للغاية، لقد قابلت ثعلباً، ثم قابلت نمراً،
وبعدها قابلت أسداً، إنهم جميعاً ينتظرونني كي يأكلونني».

At last, the old woman arrived at her daughter's house.
"Oh Daughter, what a terrible journey I've had. First I met a fox,
and then a tiger and then a lion. They're all waiting to eat me."

ردت الإبنة قائلة: «لا تقلقي يا أماه، سنفكر في حل ما، عليك ان تستريحي أولاً وتتناولي بعض الطعام».

"Don't worry Mother, we'll think of something. But first,
you must rest and have some food," answered her daughter.

بقيت المرأة العجوز مع إبنتها ثلاثة أشهر، تناولت خلالها الكثير من الطعام فأصبحت ممتلئة وجميلة.

The old woman stayed with her daughter for three months. During that time, she was given so much to eat that she became nice and fat and round.

عندما حان الوقت كي تعود المرأة العجوز الى بيتها أخذت تسأل إبنتها:
«ماذا أفعل يا إبنتي؟ كل الحيوانات تنتظرني كي تأكلني».

When it was time to go home, the old woman asked her daughter,
"What shall I do? All the animals are waiting to eat me."

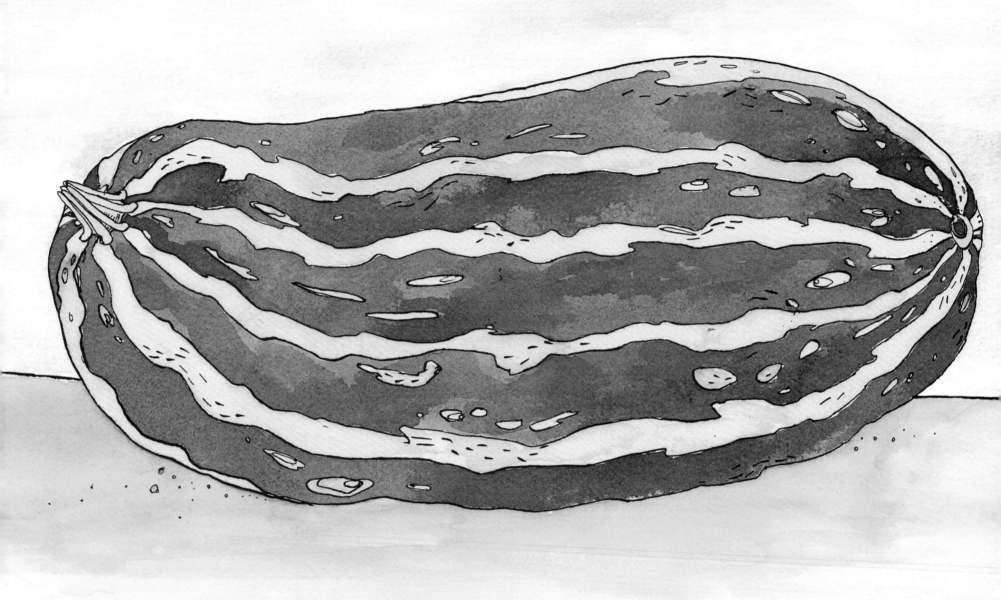

أجابت الإبنة قائلة: «هيا يا أمي لدي خطة رائعة».
ثم ذهبت الإبنة الى الحديقة وأحضرت أكبر ثمرة يقطين وجدتها هناك، وقطعتها من أعلى ثم فرغتها من الداخل.

"Come Mother, I have a plan," answered the daughter, and went into the garden. There, she picked the largest marrow she could find, cut off the top and hollowed it out.

قالت الإبنة لأمها: «هيا يا أمي إقفزي داخل ثمرة اليقطين، سوف أقوم بدفعها كي تتدحرج بك حتى تصلين الى البيت، مع السلامة يا أمي».
«مع السلامة يا إبنتي» ردت الأم وهي تحتضن إبنتها.

"Climb in. Then, I'll push the marrow, and it will roll you home. Goodbye Mother."
"Goodbye Daughter," answered the old woman, as they hugged each other.

أغلقت الإبنة ثمرة اليقطين ثم دفعتها الى الأمام.
وبينما كانت ثمرة اليقطين تتدحرج أخذت العجوز بوري تغني بصوت منخفض:
«ثمرة اليقطين تتدحرج والكل عليها يتفرج».

The daughter sealed the marrow and gave it a push.
As it rolled along, Buri sang:
"Marrow turning round and round,
We are rolling homeward bound."

عندما رأى الأسد ثمرة اليقطين تتدحرج أخذ يزمجر ويقول:
«أيتها اليقطينة، أنت كبيرة ولذيذة، ولكنني أنتظر بوري العزيزة»، ثم دفعها الى الأمام.
وبينما كانت ثمرة اليقطين تتدحرج أخذت بوري تغني:
«ثمرة اليقطين تتدحرج والكل عليها يتفرج».

When it reached the lion, he roared, "Marrow you're big and juicy,
but I'm waiting for my Buri," and he gave it a push.
As it rolled along, Buri sang:
"Marrow turning round and round,
We are rolling homeward bound."

عندما رأى النمر ثمرة اليقطين وهي تتدحرج أخذ يزمجر ويقول:
«أيتها اليقطينة، أنت كبيرة ولذيذة، ولكنني أنتظر بوري العزيزة»، ثم دفعها الى الأمام.
وبينما كانت ثمرة اليقطين تتدحرج أخذت بوري تغني:
«ثمرة اليقطين تتدحرج والكل عليها يتفرج».

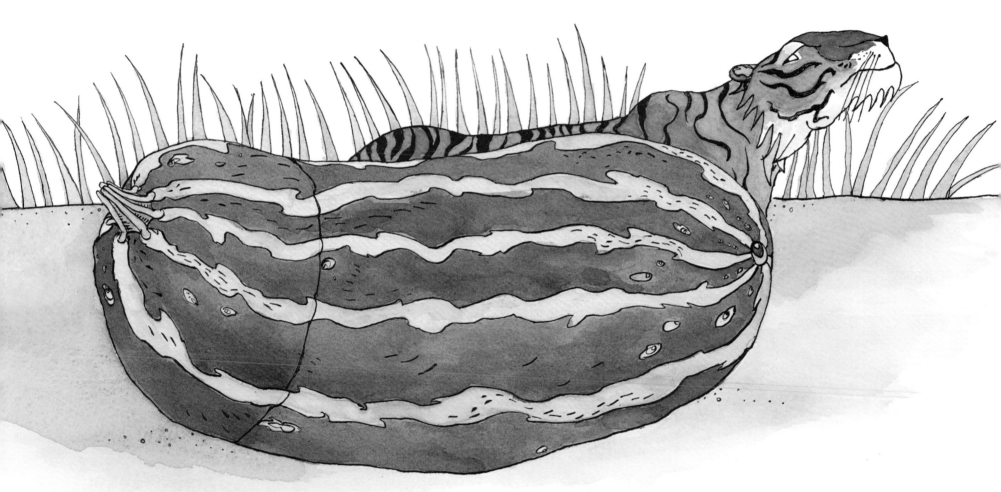

When it reached the tiger, he growled, "Marrow you're big and juicy,
but I'm waiting for my Buri," and he gave it a push.
As it rolled along, Buri sang:
"Marrow turning round and round,
We are rolling homeward bound."

لما وصلت ثمرة اليقطين الى الثعلب نظر إليها وأخذ يزمجر ويقول:
«أيتها اليقطينة، أنت كبيرة ولذيذة، ولكنني أنتظر بوري العزيزة».

But when it reached the fox, he looked at it and snarled,
"Marrow you're big and juicy, but I know you're hiding my Buri."

هجم الثعلب على ثمرة اليقطين ومزقها فوجد المرأة العجوز داخلها.
أخذ الثعلب يزمجر ويقول: «بوري بوري، سوف آكُلكِ الآن».

And the fox pounced onto the marrow and tore it apart. Inside, he found the old woman.
"Buri, Buri, I'm going to eat you now," he snarled.

أخذت العجوز تتوسل الى الثعلب وتقول: «أيها الثعلب، أتوسل إليك أن تتركني حتى أرى بيتي مرة ثانية، وبعد ذلك يمكنك أن تأكلني».
رد الثعلب قائلاً: «سوف أتركك يا بوري حتى ترين بيتك».

"Oh fox, before you eat me, please let me see
my home again," pleaded the old woman.
"Buri, Buri, I WILL let you see your home,"
said the fox.

ولما وصلت بوري الى البيت أخذت تصرخ وتقول:
«لالو، النجدة... النجدة!».
خرج الكلبان مسرعين وأخذا يطاردان الثعلب حتى
فرّ هارباً وابتعد.

When they reached the old woman's house, she screamed,
"Lalu! Bhalu! Save me! Save me!"
The two big dogs raced out of the house and chased
the fox, who ran and ran until he got away.

ثم وقف الثعلب يتحسر ويقول: «لقد غلبتني يا بوري، كل ما لدي الآن هو ثمرة اليقطين لأضعها في الشاي».
أما المرأة العجوز، فإنها لم تشاهد الثعلب مرة أخرى، وعاشت سعيدة في بيتها.

When he stopped, he sighed, "Buri, Buri, you got the better of me.
Now, all I have is marrow for my tea."
As for the old woman, she was never troubled by the fox again.

For
Chabi Dutta whose telling of the story inspired this book.
H.B.

For

my mum and dad, with love.
L.F.

Buri and the Marrow is a Bengali folk tale. The word *Buri* means *old woman* in Bengali

Mantra Lingua Ltd
Global House, 303 Ballards Lane, London N12 8NP
www.mantralingua.com

First published in 2000 by Mantra Lingua
This edition 2012
Text copyright © 2000 Henriette Barkow
Dual Language Text copyright © 2000 Mantra Lingua
Illustrations copyright © 2000 Lizzie Finlay

A CIP record for this book is available from the British Library